Further Whispers of Hope

Jennifer René Daniel

Conjurske Publications
Rhinelander, WI   2015

©2015 by Jennifer René Daniel.
All rights reserved. Published 2015.
ISBN-13: 978-1-935923-01-5

Conjurske Publications
3215 County Rd G
Rhinelander, WI 54501
www.conjurskepublications.com

Conjurske Publications gratefully acknowledges the use of the Database of Mid-Victorian Engraving, compiled by Cardiff University, for all illustrations included in this book.

The Authorized King James Version was used for all Scripture verses quoted in this text.

Front cover painting by Enid le Roux.

Printed in the United States of America.

*This book is dedicated to my parents,
Jannie and Enid le Roux.*

Contents

SALVATION 1
    What Is the Worth of Riches? 2
    Repentance 3
    Such Were Some of You................................ 4
    The Rock of Salvation 6
    Thou, the Answer 7
    Be of Good Cheer! 8
    I'm Confident 11

CHRISTIAN LIVING 13
    Lord, I Am Shy 14
    Life Is So Busy 15
    'Twas Just a Whisper of Satan 16
    It's Easier 18
    Unto the Pure 19
    My Motives 20
    My Tongue Today 21
    As a Hen 22
    Don't Push Me from the Nest 23
    They Keep Their Garments Pure 24
    They Point a Finger at Me 26
    Don't Go and Ask My Family 27
    Add to Your Faith... 28
    It Is Not 30
    I Leave This Child with Thee 31
    Life and Death 32
    A Haunting Melody 34
    I'll Fight the Enemies 36
    Patience Towards Others 37
    Growing in Grace 38
    It's Hard to Control Your Temper 39
    God's Mirror 40

We Can't 41
　　Prayer Is an Earnest Warfare 42
　　The Extra Mile 43

Consecration 45
　　At the Brink of the Day 46
　　My Focus 48
　　I Should Be First! 49
　　Hearken to Me, Oh Daughter 50
　　The King Desires Your Beauty 52
　　His Yoke 53

Encouragement 55
　　Laden with Burdens 56
　　This Year I Lost My Confidence 57
　　Why Was I Ever Born? 58
　　I'm Despondent 60
　　Her Cry 61
　　Confidence Gone 62
　　Though He Slay Me 64
　　How Could God Send These Trials? 65
　　Sinking Child 66
　　Can Thy Word Still Be Fulfilled? 68
　　Child, Are You Laden with Burdens? 70
　　Under His Wings 71
　　I See a Person Bending 72
　　Are You a Wandering Pilgrim? 73
　　I Need Not Fear 74
　　My Saviour Is Beside Me 76
　　My Feet Had Wandered 77
　　A Prayer Became a Cry 78
　　Be Not Afraid 80
　　Thy God Looks After Thee 82
　　My Delight 83
　　Submission 84
　　Does My Faith Falter? 86
　　Patience 87

Failure & Repentance 89
Friendship with the World 90
I Did Not Take the Time........................... 91
Disobedience 92
Why Should I Not Be First? 93
No Room for God, Oh Christian 94
Bitterness 95
I Used to Trust Thy Word.......................... 96
My Confidence Has Slipped........................ 98
Dear Lord..100
Too Proud, Child of Mine..........................101
I Took a Little Sin.................................102
It Started Subtly 103
Unkind 104
My Protection....................................105
My Great Failure..................................106
Things Have Gone Wrong..........................108
This Modern World 110
Why Should I Make an Effort? 111
Voices Keep Calling God's Children.................112
I Murmured 114
Too Great Is the Cost..............................115
Ashamed! 116
Sadly Lacking 117

The Christian's Calling 119
The Poor Man....................................120
Satan's Legions 122
Have You Purposed? 123
There Is No Better Time 124
I Always Dreamt..................................125
Ambassador 126
The Breastplate...................................127
I Had Left Thy Sword 128
This Morning 129
God Has Equipped Us 130
The World Is Ever Clinging........................131

I See the Enemy 132
Oh, Dangerous to Go Right In 133
The Battle Is a Fierce One 134

JUDGMENT & THE UNSAVED 135
Too Proud 136
You Spurned My Love 137
No Room — the Agnostic and Sceptic 138
Procrastination 139
At the Judgment Seat 140
No Room 142

STORIES FROM SCRIPTURE 143
Shadrach, Meshach, Abednego 144
Dark Clouds Around Daniel 145
Among the Shouting Crowd 146
When I Look at Peter 148
Hannah and Samuel's Coat 150
The Lord Has Answered Prayer 151
Let Us Pull Out the Tares 152
Leah Was Not Beautiful 154
A Child Ambassador 155
The Samaritan Woman 156

Dear Reader,

We live in a world that has sunk into despair. Physical, environmental, and man-made calamities confront mankind across the globe. So many, bravely smiling, are trapped in personal misery. People have disappointed us, hopes have been smashed, and the future is dark.

May *Further Whispers of Hope* reach you where you are and point you to God whose "peace passeth all understanding" and who has promised "never to leave, nor forsake" those who belong to Him.

This is my prayer,

Jennifer R. Daniel

Salvation

As the out-flung rope to the drowning swimmer, the beckoning light to the weary traveler, the casting off of an insupportable weight to the stumbling straggler, salvation is our only anchor and safeguard in the storms of life!

What Is the Worth of Riches?

What is the worth of riches
    Before God's judgment throne?
Worthless against salvation
    Hear the young ruler's moan

"Why did I turn and leave Christ?
    The day He said to me
'Sell your goods' I refused Him
    Lost for eternity."

The woman cried, "I have found Him
    He offered me water true
It became a living fountain
    Christ did my heart renew."

God holds out His forgiveness
    At a moment of your life
You can turn and spurn His offer
    Or accept His sacrifice

Repentance

Dear Father, I bow in repentance
    In sorrow I come unto Thee
For years I have spurned Thy salvation
    Sin was too attractive to me

But now I accept Thy salvation
    Forgiveness for all that I've done
I humbly accept Thy great offer
    Thy pardon for me, worthless one

Such Were Some of You

"Know ye not that the unrighteous shall not inherit the kingdom of God? Be not deceived: neither fornicators, nor idolaters, nor adulterers, nor effeminate, nor abusers of themselves with mankind, Nor thieves, nor covetous, nor drunkards, nor revilers, nor extortioners, shall inherit the kingdom of God. And such were some of you: but ye are washed, but ye are sanctified, but ye are purified, but ye are justified in the name of the Lord Jesus, and by the Spirit of our God." 1 Cor. 6:9–11

> He's fallen far too low, they say
>   For God to rescue him
> Just look at all the things he's done
>   The places he has been
>
> And yet we read in God's own Word
>   Of murderous, evil men
> Who grasped God's outstretched hand of love
>   And rose above sin's den
>
> We read of men, effeminate
>   Abusers with mankind
> Who too in deep repentance
>   Did God's deliverance find
>
> For doth the Scripture not proclaim
>   That such were some of you?
> It points to God's own grace that reached
>   The outcast sinners too

God doth not make exceptions
   Or categories of sin
His love reached down from Calvary
   Each sinking child to win

The list is rather fearful
   Of what their lives had been
Until the precious blood of Christ
   Had washed such sinners clean

The word *were* is delightful
   It wipes out all the past
And states that sin which claimed men's lives
   By God's grace need not last

For He had wiped the stains away
   The guilt and crippling shame
They thus in garments pure and white
   Will conquer in God's name

But note, *were* doth not indicate
   That sin sustains its hold
Their lives were changed—a different walk
   Within the Master's fold

And so let us not judge the past
   If Christ has paid the price
To cleanse and change man's wicked soul
   And wipe out every vice

The Rock of Salvation

The Rock of Salvation is higher than I
    Only the Lamb could God's wrath satisfy
Sinless and spotless, His blood, substitute
    Rock of Salvation—on cross rough and rude

Ah Rock of Salvation, Thou higher than I
    Lift me from sin—'tis to Thee that I cry
Only Thy hands pierced could reach me indeed
    Only Thy arms lift me up in my need

Thou, the Answer

War and bloodshed, death, despair
   Deep, depressive world of care
Sordid darkness, choking night
   Sinking downwards without light

Light of Heaven, shine below
   Through the darkness send Thy glow
Let the needy world perceive
   Thou, the answer to their need

Thou, a baby—fragile, small
   Came to give Thy life, Thy all
God an infant, can it be
   He would leave His heaven for me?

Reaching out, not to condemn
   Ah, the love poured out to men
For man's soul to justify
   Christ for his sin came to die!

BE OF GOOD CHEER!
"Son, be of good cheer; thy sins be forgiven thee."
Matt. 9:2b

Sick of the palsy—the poor man
  So fragile, spent, and weak
Unable to stand up and walk
  His future very bleak

But friends can be the means God takes
  To reach a fallen man
Those friends who longed that he'd be healed
  Were in God's sovereign plan!

Christ mentioned that He saw their faith
  How precious that it brought
The burdened man right to the Lord
  For Him, salvation wrought

For Christ immediately cried out
  "Be of good cheer, I say
Your sin—the 'burden of your heart'
  Forgiven on this day!

What matters that you cannot walk
    Dependent on your friends
Your very soul for this alone
    Cries out; your sore heart rends."

How sceptical the scornful crowd
    As they Christ's words despise
Rather an outward miracle
    Before their very eyes

To prove His right, God condescends
    To make this weak man walk
Salvation undisputed
    Countered their scornful talk

Christ comes to every one of us
    By means He chooses to
As we stand in His presence
    What will we say and do?

What is the longing of our heart
    Mere bodily relief?
Or has the burden of our sin
    Filled our sad hearts with grief?

'Tis only when Christ's blessed words
    Have reached into our soul
"Forgiven—Be of cheer, My child
    I've come to make you whole!"

That life reaches a higher plane
    I'm in the Master's hands
No longer struggling blindly on
    I walk where He has planned

Thus it is joy to live, to be
    My life with purpose filled
Forgiveness, sweet and precious, has
    My turmoil quelled and stilled!

I'm Confident

I'm confident that on the cross
    My Saviour paid the price
A holy God demanded
    For mankind's sin and vice

I'm confident that Jesus' blood
    Can wash away my sin
That through His death and sacrifice
    His pardon I will win

CHRISTIAN LIVING

Day by Day

LORD, I AM SHY

Lord, I am so shy that I
    Should really be excused
Others are more competent
    For Thee, dear Lord, to use

Moses felt he couldn't speak
    Thy mouthpiece could not be
Thus Aaron was the spokesman sent
    Who spoke so fluently

Yet if I should consider
    The path that Aaron went
The calves he made the people serve
    The criticism lent

Moses despite his stammering tongue
    Would not have led astray
The disobedient Israelites
    Upon the desert way

It is not only competence
    Or talents by the score
Obedience is more paramount
    By Thee—considered more!

Life Is So Busy

Life is so busy, no time for much prayer
    I am just running and filled with despair
Food preparation and schoolwork and more
    I am not coping, to God a closed door

Surely, dear Father, Thou wilt understand
    No time to serve Thee the way I had planned
Life's gained momentum and I've drowned therein
    Perhaps that's the reason I dabbled with sin

No room for Jesus is dangerous ground
    No room for Jesus is bound to confound
Without His help, burdens increase in weight
    Don't keep the door closed until it's too late

Don't be too busy to seek Him in prayer
    Busy with pots? You can still meet Him there
Schoolwork and study will soon better grow
    If you let Jesus direct them below

'Twas Just a Whisper of Satan

'Twas just a whisper of Satan
    Into the ears of Eve
Causing her faith to falter
    That did her heart deceive

Subtle suggestions from Satan
    Follow us every day
Making us doubt His promise
    Crippling us on our way

He'll undermine God's power
    Question that He could be
True to His Word and faithful
    Within adversity

Jesus said, "I'll not leave you"
    Satan says, "He has left"
Striving to pierce faith's armour
    Leaving God's child bereft

Joy, peace, and trust unchanging
    Childlike dependency
Can with a whisper from Satan
    Flee and depart from thee

Thus, child of God, don't heed him
    Spurn Satan's subtle voice
You need not be his victim
    Unless it is by choice!

It's Easier

It's easier to be a light
    To people far away
Than to be a constant witness
    To the home folks every day

The pressure keeps on mounting
    The anger in me boils
Behind closed doors I'm failing
    The family recoils

Ah Lord, I've let Thy calling
    Fall down, escape from me
I did not see my mission
    Was to my family

Unto the Pure

Unto the pure, all things are pure?
    It seems to be untrue
For in a world of sin and wrong
    Things gain an impure hue

But to the pure who shun the wrong
    And flee from sin and vice
Who keep their garments spotless white
    This statement doth suffice

Their eyes are fixed upon a home
    That is not of the earth
They covet not the transient wealth
    Of no eternal worth

They do not isolate themselves
    While they souls seek to win
Rather they walk within the world
    Keeping themselves from sin

My Motives

Lord, am I seeking the well-done of others
    When I am being benevolent, kind?
What is my motive behind the good actions?
    There in the innermost, what dost Thou find?

Is it a heart that is full of compassion,
    Selfless in seeking a soul to relieve?
"Only for others" my burning incentive
    Or is there pride that can injure and grieve?

Ah, Blessed Saviour, I tasted forgiveness
    Love so unmeasured—beyond human ken
Let me in gratitude show real compassion
    If I would lost ones to Thee ever win!

My Tongue Today

What has my tongue set forth today?
    Kindness that smoothed another's way?
Was it a harsh and biting word
    Or was my tongue with pity stirred?

As a Hen
Matthew 23:37

The farmyard is a happy scene of noises
    The hen, contented, chuckles with her brood
When swift o'erhead dark wings begin to hover
    As swift, the hen—alert doth change her mood

She cries aloud an urgent, stringent warning
    She calls and pleads, "Come right unto my side"
Her wings outstretched to shelter all her chickens
    "Come nearer chicks; beneath these you can hide."

But one small chick doth wander on unheeding
    He does not see the shadow sweeping low
"Why should I heed the call? there is no danger"
    And then his body crumples 'neath the blow

Dear Saviour, let me not be deaf to warnings
    To wander off, despite Thy urgent call
I would not be the chick in the hawk's talons
    Under Thy wings my only shelt'ring wall

Don't Push Me from the Nest

Don't push me from the nest
    Where all is safe and sound
For then I'll plummet downwards
    Towards the hard stone ground

I'll dash against the rocks
    I'll be a crumpled mess
And thus I cling and hold
    Refusing Thy request

I feel a rush of wind
    As from the nest I fall
Tremulously trusting
    Thou canst hear my call

Thy mighty wings are outspread
    Beneath this weak fledgling
Thus the "fragile" rises
    Soars, begins to sing

They Keep Their Garments Pure

"...neither be partaker of other men's sins: keep thyself pure." 1 Tim. 5:22b

Unto the pure, all things are pure
For they do look upon
The true, the good, the innocent
And shun all sin and wrong

Unto the pure, all things are pure
For since the world's begun
Within its sordid boundaries
From evil they will run

E'en in the depths of darkness
   They see God's glimmering light
They know God's intervention
   Will help them do what's right

With sadness, sorrow, hardship
   They know God rules above
And in the time appointed
   He'll show His hand of love

There's much not comprehended
    Upon this earthly sphere
But looking unto Heaven
    They wait to see it clear

With face like flint, faced upwards
    They keep their garments pure
And so despite the onslaughts
    They'll survive and endure

They Point a Finger at Me

They point a finger at me, dear Lord
    Accused me loud and clear
Of sin I'd never stoop to
    Their cries filled me with fear

They point a finger at me, dear Lord
    And say that I have lied
Ah, see my misery and grief
    The tears that I have cried

They point a finger at Thee, dear Lord
    But Thou didst not reply
But rather turned the other cheek
    To each accusing lie

If I would Christ's disciple be
    I too will be accused
Taunted and mocked—ridiculed
    Like Him too, be abused

Dear God, before Thy throne I yield
    My life, what it doth hold
Take me and let me be Thy slave
    As if I had been sold

Don't Go and Ask My Family

Don't go and ask my family
    About my Christian walk
Thank goodness they are silent folks
    What if the girls should talk?

It's safe to lose my temper there
    To be both cruel and mean
As long as no one hears of it
    Or nothing has been seen!

But child, the home is paramount
    It tests reality
You're real if you are really real
    Within the family

Add to Your Faith...
2 Peter 1:5–8

It's possible that I may be
    Blind, stumbling on my way
Because addition was not thought
    Essential for each day

Although I grasped the rope of faith
    Was saved by God's own grace
Addition did not follow
    Thus stumbling in the race

For after faith comes virtue
    Essential for each one
To live out her salvation
    In all that's said and done

Work out your own salvation
    My sheep will follow Me
Obedience is the keystone
    Into eternity

Then comes the word called temperance
    To keep yourself in hand
Keeping your temper constant
    Doing as God hath planned

And then the next essential
    Patience upon your way
To bear with other's failings
    To trust God hath full sway

The next stage in addition
    Is godliness, for you
Will become more like Jesus
    In all you think and do

Of course kindness is part of
    The great addition call
To reach out to your brother
    To lift those who may fall

When you have reached the goalpost
    Of adding on your way
Love will be the virtue
    That crowns all else that day!

It Is Not

It is not where you go today
    But if it is God's will
That will allow His wondrous peace
    Your very soul to fill

It is not that you're working hard
    And labouring each day
But whether burdens you absorb
    God placed upon your way

I Leave This Child with Thee

Lord, I leave this child with Thee
    His will I do not own
In his frail hands, the vital choice
    If he will God disown?

But I can follow him in prayer
    Surround him with my love
Show him what's in Thy Word, dear Lord
    Point him to heaven above

Lord, I must leave this child with Thee
    I place him in Thy care
Knowing Thy Holy Spirit will
    Bid him of sin beware

Trembling, I wait and watch, dear Lord
    Trusting that he will come
Turning from sin to find in Thee
    Earth's battles fought and won

Life and Death

Life and death in the tongue's mighty grip
    In a short moment it turns to a whip
Where sweet encouragement is in dire need
    It rather breaks down, that sufferers bleed

In a short second a life has been slain
    Not in the battlefield out on the plain
But in the thoughts which the tongue has put in
    There on the pathway where its feet have been

Ah, what destruction doth lie in the tongue
    Lost are the battles that could have been won
Brothers and sisters and parents will say
    The tongue has crippled them so much today

But what encouragement lies in the tongue!
    How many battles through it can be won
How many people get up when they fall
    Because sweet counsel was there at their call

See a tired mother look up with a smile
    Because of "Thank you" said once in a while
See the old granny that chuckles with glee
    Because a grandchild listened patiently

Sometimes a Scripture encouragement brings
    Lifting the spirit and strengthening wings
Sometimes it's just a kind word said with care
    That helps another his burdens to bear

A Haunting Melody

In the midst of all the clamour
    That a Christmas season brings
There is a haunting melody
    Which in the chaos rings

It speaks of God's compassion
    His boundless love and grace
A manger with a baby small
    To save the human race

It points to His perfection
    As the chosen Lamb of God
As countless steps are chronicled
    Upon the path He trod

It whispers of the price He paid
   While on the cross He hung
Our sins upon His body laid
   He our forgiveness won

It laughs that death was powerless
   To keep Him prisoner
Triumphant He arose on high
   Our Mighty Conqueror

And thus amidst the turmoil
   Of the Christmas holiday
There is a haunting melody
   That blesses me each day

I'll Fight the Enemies

No room for pride or arrogance
  Suspicion, envy, fear
Those enemies are vanquished
  If My sword is always near

For faithful is the Word of God
  To stop the tempter's thrust
Because its steel is tempered by
  The words "In God we trust!"

Patience Towards Others

When little babies cannot walk
    We smile and say, "One day
They'll be running us out of breath
    Just wait and see!" we say

When little babies cannot talk
    And merely smile and pout
We smile and say, "They'll soon converse
    And even scream and shout!"

We know that it takes time to learn
    To grow into a man
Their baby steps and stuttering words
    We excuse, understand

And yet we are impatient
    When converts are quite new
And don't do all the very things
    We think that they should do

We do not show them patience
    Remembering that we
Were once too a mere baby
    Growing steadily!

Growing in Grace

How sad when Christians do not care
    To grow in grace each day
They do not seek those higher heights
    God sets out on their way

Instead of striving to please God
    More Christlike to become
They remain little babies
    And stay where they've begun

IT'S HARD TO CONTROL YOUR TEMPER

It's hard to control your temper
    When you know you are right
It's far easier to end up
    In a huge, verbal fight

It's hard to be the least, when
    Others force you to do
The things that they neglected
    And dump it onto you

It's hard to listen quietly
    To one who thinks her words
Are full of wisdom, when they
    Are boring and absurd

It's hard to hold in anger
    When people hurt and jab
When every word they utter
    Enters like a deep stab

But self-control is vital
    To keep your witness bright
At home, at work, on all fields
    Essential to stay bright

God's Mirror

Why don't you peep in God's mirror today
    See what it shows up; the truth will have sway
See there the blemishes shown from God's Word
    So that, by looking, your conscience is stirred

Selfishness, anger, and pride hover there
    Marring your image; your beauty impair
For all the blemishes shown in God's light
    Show you that they will your loveliness blight

Look in God's mirror, digest what you see
    Let God remove all the blotches from thee
Daily return to observe where you are
    To see the blotches that your visage mar!

We Can't

We can't force our loved ones to follow God
    But we cover them in prayer
Thus our love will rise to the Throne of Grace
    And meet the Saviour there

We can't follow feet upon the earth
    When ours have feebler grown
But our prayers run ahead and reach God's ear
    Each cry a heart-rent groan

We can't fill the pitfalls that lie in wait
    For a loved one to fall in
But our cry to God can let His voice
    Confront them in their sin

Prayer Is an Earnest Warfare

Prayer is an earnest warfare
With Satan as our foe
Fought in the realms of heaven
And on the earth below

God gives His children armour
To equip them for prayer
He knows that Satan's arrows
Will fall upon them there

The Extra Mile

Love lets me walk the extra mile
    And turn the other cheek
Love lets me temper what I say
    Into an answer meek

Love lets me seek in word and deed
    To rather be the least
In all things seeking God's "Well done"
    Until all toil is ceased

Of all the virtues given
    Love makes up the whole sum
For Love is their reflection
    Blending them into one

CONSECRATION

"I beseech you therefore, brethren, by the mercies of God, that ye present your bodies a living sacrifice, holy, acceptable unto God, which is your reasonable service.

And be not conformed to this world: but be ye transformed by the renewing of your mind, that ye may prove what is that good, and acceptable, and perfect, will of God."

Romans 12:1–2

AT THE BRINK OF THE DAY

At the brink of the day, His tender voice
    Seemed to whisper unto me
I need your limbs, your heart, your mind
    To heed me faithfully

Not in the halls of fame, dear child
    Nor for the crowd's applause
But in the home with all its chores
    Yes dear, behind closed doors

At the brink of the day, when I rush to work
    In an alien, godless crowd
I seem to hear God's earnest voice
    Above the tumult loud

I need your light to shine, dear child
    Within your earthly sphere
Your word, your acts, your attitude
    Can bring My presence near

At the brink of the day, as I rush to school
    With my mind on problems bent
I seem to hear a whispering
    "How will your day be spent?"

Your friends at school—a mission field
    They seek reality
And you, My child, can show them that
    'Tis only found in Me

My Focus

How can I let my focus
Be other than the Lord?
He should be first and foremost
By me obeyed, adored

Who else left heaven's glory
Came to the earth to die
So that He could redeem us
Mankind to justify

His will is first and foremost
To Him, I give my all
My eyes on Him are focused
I will obey His call

Jesus, I am Thy servant
To serve Thee every day
To do what Thou desireth
Each step upon life's way

I Should Be First!

I should be first in your heart, dear child
    None other rise above
To claim your first allegiance
    And capture all your love

I should be first in your heart, dear child
    Decisions that you make
Should not be those that grieve My heart
    E'en for a loved one's sake

I should be first in your heart, dear child
    None other God but Me
I claim your sole allegiance
    Into eternity

Hearken to Me, Oh Daughter

Hearken to Me, oh daughter
    Yes, hear your heavenly King
Forget thy father's people
    And to My being cling

I see in you rare beauty
    I long to save your soul
To take you—broken vessel
    And make you truly whole

You too, oh erring daughter
    Who failed so publicly
Do not allow the devil
    To rob and cripple thee

For he would scar your beauty
    And rob you of your crown
Defile your golden garments
    And keep your spirits down

Rise up, oh kingly daughter
    Receive My pardon true
Reflect My grace and beauty
    That I your soul renew

Thy daughter bows in reverence
    Submits to Thee, oh King
Her heart, her life, her being
    She doth with gladness bring

The King Desires Your Beauty

The King desires your beauty
To spread His loving grace
To radiate His sweetness
Through you in every place

Submit, oh kingly daughter
To be His instrument
Your beauty, His endowing
His work to complement

Within, His glorious working
Flows forth to beautify
Your works, your words, your being
Your God to glorify

HIS YOKE

I bow and say, Put on Thy yoke
    According to Thy will
I'll go wherever Thou dost bid
    With joy my path fulfill

I do not ask to see ahead
    I cannot raise my head
For while beneath Thy yoke, we can
    But see one step ahead

Although it be the mountain crags
    The storms or valleys deep
I'll just plod on beneath Thy yoke
    Knowing I'm in Thy keep

'Tis only then I'll learn what Thou
    Ordained in love for me
Submissive and compliant
    To what was sent by Thee!

Therefore I bow and say, "Dear Lord
    Put on Thy yoke today
Willing, I'll carry all its weight
    Within the narrow way!"

Encouragement

A drop of water to the thirsty, a smile to the lonely, a word of encouragement to the weary, a helping hand to the fallen, a glimmer of light in the darkness of despair!

LADEN WITH BURDENS

Laden with burdens, men sink in despair
    Life is a struggle; they're burdened with care
Leaden the sky as they cry out in vain
    No one will answer and deaden the pain

Some seek to please God, but fail to find peace
    Trying and trying, their efforts don't cease
Crushed by the knowledge that task is too great
    They dread life's journey, their ultimate fate!

Though Christ had called out to all lost in sin
    Though He had died their salvation to win
Still they plod on, close their ears to His call
    No joy or peace in existence at all!

But other Christians who rail and complain
    Against God's dealings again and again
Life is so dark, they have embraced despair
    Their weary cry: "Surely God does not care!"

But there are others who lean on the Lord
    He gave them strength and their courage restored
The way still steep, but with help from above
    His yoke is easy because of His love!

This Year I Lost My Confidence

This year I lost my confidence
    In God; His love, His care
So that I stumbled on the path
    My helpmeet was "Despair"

I seemed to hear a gentle voice
    That bids me look on high
To see the jagged, rugged path
    Is leading to the sky

Lift up, lift up your confidence
    And see your God above
The storms, the trials, the tragedies
    He reigneth, child, with love

Why Was I Ever Born?

What am I doing here?
    Why was I ever born?
Life's filled with so much sorrow
    My path with many a thorn

Is there a purpose for my life
    A plan for little me?
I'm drowning midst the multitudes
    That are humanity

Ah child, my dearest, precious one
    You're here to do My will
There is a plan that in this world
    I would have you fulfill

For you, I shed My precious blood
    To cleanse and save your soul
For firstly, child, initially
    I need to make you whole

And thus I ask that you would give
    To Me yourself, your all
Don't leave the best lamb hidden
    And harboured in your stall!

My plan for you holds little things
    You need to do each day
Each task a vital link that I
    Require upon life's way

Look up—beyond the daily toil
    To heaven further on
For then you'll find its radiance shines
    On all you've said and done

Endure, my child, what I may send
    On your allotted way
Don't flinch and run, but persevere
    My strength is there each day

What am I doing here? Praise God
    What He requires of me
A pilgrim on the heaven-bound way
    To God's eternity

I'm Despondent

Ah Lord, I am despondent
    In circumstances bleak
I'm losing trust and sinking
    Thy presence I must seek

The battle is the Captain's
    He'll conquer every foe
If He is at the forefront
    He'll counter every blow!

HER CRY

No one understands, dear Lord
    My heaviness of soul
The sickness that has crippled me
    The yearning for console

No one understands, dear Lord
    My loneliness, despair
As I battle private woes
    Not a sign of care

No one understands, dear Lord
    What I crave fulfilled
Human comfort has not once
    My great heartache stilled

No one understands—but Thee
    Comforter and Friend
Ah what bliss, Thy sympathy
    Doth my heartache mend!

Thus Thy understanding
    Makes my burden light
For what Thou appointest
    I know must be right!

Confidence Gone

Ah Lord, I lost my confidence
    When sickness took her hold
I doubted Thy omnipotence
    Pain made my trust grow cold

I could not understand, dear Lord
    Why I should suffer so
As sensing my receding strength
    My state has laid me low

The woman in the Bible times
    Was healed, the blind could see
And thus it seems so cruel, dear Lord
    That Thou dost not heal me

But then I seemed to hear Thy voice
    That said, "Child, I love thee
My arms are underneath you
    If you would only see!

'Twas love that chose your path of pain
    It was the only way
That I could draw you closer
    Embrace you every day."

And thus I will not cast away
    My blessed confidence
One day in God's own heaven
    'Twill all make perfect sense

Though He Slay Me...

"Though he slay me, yet will I trust in him: but I will maintain mine own ways before him." Job 13:15

The Christians in the dread arena
    Faced death in many different ways
Their bodies torn and cleft asunder
    Bestrewed with blood within those days

Yet in the fires, they trusted in the covert
    Of wings almighty covering them in love
They did not doubt a loving God's compassion
    Though tortured, slain, He ruled above

I too may face the lions of Satan's anger
    Where tongues will slay and opposition fell
But I too trust that He is there beside me
    His wings my cover, and thus all is well

How Could God Send These Trials?

How could God send these trials to me?
How can I pass this test?
It seems more difficult than those
Allotted to the rest

How can God hold the universe
Within His mighty hand
And yet allow the things that I
Just cannot understand?

Ah child, if you had confidence
In God Who ruleth all
You would not let the trials and tests
Cause you to stumble, fall

One day when time has ended
And this earth's labour's past
You'll understand the reason
Rejoice in God at last

Sinking Child

Ah sinking, fainting child of mine
    I hear your plaintive cry
As there beneath the pressing loads
    Your bruised, weak form doth lie

You think the promises are void
    Of ever coming true
You feel as if 'tis mockery
    To trust in them anew

You do not have the strength to call
    Your faith has been destroyed
It seems another life when you
    God's promises enjoyed

You cannot rise above the storm
    You cannot meet the need
You cannot pass the stringent tests
    Your Saviour hath decreed

But child, the apple of God's eye
    You are His constant care
You are the one He'll lift aloft
    And on His shoulders bear

He is your God in Heaven
    He is omniscient
He is the great Provider
    Your God omnipotent

Can Thy Word Still Be Fulfilled?

Oh, can Thy Word still be fulfilled?
    With fear, my courage has been stilled
I cannot hope—I cannot see
    How Thou canst make it true for me

But perfect love should not instill
    Fears, doubts, beneath God's perfect will
For His own Word can never fail
    Despite the storms, it will prevail

Ah Lord, a loved one went astray
    Alone I cry, in deep dismay
Can Thou o'ercome my wounded grief
    Can she repent—I find relief?

My child, when hearts do still My voice
    And turn from Me, they seal their choice
Their pleasures will be bitter gall
    'Twixt Me and them, sin's dreadful wall

My Word will fall upon their way
    To call them out from sin's dread sway
But you, dear hurt and floundering one
    Must lean more fully on God's Son

My love is there to comfort you
    My peace will bid you hope anew
Thy God, Who sees each sparrow's fall
    Will heed thy faintest cry or call

Child, Are You Laden with Burdens?

Child, are you laden with burdens
    That are not sent down by Me?
Crippled and failing, you struggle
    Losing your bright testimony

Roll all those burdens upon Me
    Seek to do only My will
Don't let unnecessary pressure
    Your life o'erwhelmingly fill

Under His Wings

"...hide me under the shadow of thy wings," Psalm 17:8b

Oh wind-tossed child, bedraggled, weak, and weary
    Who walks in stubbornness, a self-willed path
You cannot meet the tempest that is brewing
    Or labour through its dreaded aftermath

Why did you leave the shelter of My presence?
    Why did you scuttle from My sheltering wing?
Will you alone face enemy and danger
    Or will My call, you to My presence bring?

"Under My wings" though dark the rending heavens
    "Under My wings" though foes would peck and kill
"Under My wings" the only place of safety
    "Under My wings"—it is the Saviour's will

I See a Person Bending

I see a person bending
    Beneath a heavy load
So many *why's* and *wherefore's*
    Within that burden stowed

But outstretched hands are waiting
    Within each laden day
A whispering voice is pleading
    Upon her burdened way

I'll change the *why's* and *wherefore's*
    Into "God's will be done"
My child, when they are lifted
    'Tis half the battle won!

The load is so much lighter
    The path more smooth ahead
When God carries your burden
    Supports the weight of lead

Are You a Wandering Pilgrim?

Are you a wandering pilgrim
    Lost in the dark land "Despair"
Fearing imag'nary tyrants
    Waiting to seize you right there?

Are you despondent and timid
    Fearful to trust in the Lord
While Christ's grace fully sufficient
    On you His strength can be poured

You must not tremble at giants
    You must not fear in the throng
God, the Omnipotent, reigneth
    In Him you too can be strong

I Need Not Fear

My feet are dragging forward
    With reluctance, precious Lord
For all the loads of yesteryear
    Upon my back are poured

Instead of leaning hard on Thee
    And finding strength to face
The challenges each day will bring
    I falter in the race

The enemy is whispering
    A darkened future, Lord
Instead of shutting up my ears
    I've his suggestions stored

And so it is a faltering child
    That comes at brink of year
To say—forgive my failures, Lord
    My lack of faith and fear

I lift my visage heavenwards
    Eternity I see
I know amidst life's trivial trials
    I'm marching, but to Thee

I need not fear the future, Lord
    It rests within Thy hand
And thus with confidence I tread
    The path that Thou hast planned

My Saviour Is Beside Me

My Saviour is beside me
    In this, life's stormy sea
Although the waves rise higher
    They do not frighten me

For He can still the tempest
    The port is known to Him
And through the darkest onslaught
    The Captain's craft has been

I'm filled with peace in knowing
    The Captain steers the ship
Therefore the boat will progress
    The rudder will not slip!

My Feet Had Wandered

It seemed my feet had wandered
    On an awesome precipice
Yet the winding path leads upwards
    And my footsteps dare not miss

There are looming clouds of darkness
    There are wailing cries of woe
Still the winding path leads upwards
    And I know I there must go

I can hear the saved ones singing
    Of their journey here below
I can hear my Master calling
    For His voice I surely know

Thus I put my feet more firmly
    And I gaze on Him alone
For I know that He'll uphold me
    'Till my pathway reaches home

A Prayer Became a Cry

The load has come with passing years
    A prayer became a cry
Where e'er I go—the burden's there
    'Midst a depressing sigh

I smile, I laugh within the crowd
    My burdens deep within
A heartache gnawing at my side
    'Midst all the clamour, din

But someone knew and saw my pain
    He tenderly stood by
He would not force His sympathy
    But lingered ever nigh

One day when life seemed dark indeed
    And far too hard to bear
I chanced to hear His soft-drawn sigh
    Ah—when will you draw near?

Child, let this load rest in My hand
    It is too hard to bear
What wondrous joy when He did take
    My burdens in His care

The load is yet a heavy one
    And yet my back is free
For Jesus came and took it up
    He bears my load for me

BE NOT AFRAID
Matthew 14

The waves around my craft soar high
    The winds lash at its side
The boat topples; I fear that I
    Cannot in it abide

Why was I sent upon this course?
    Does God not care at all?
Does He not sense how weak I am,
    How frightened in the squall?

The sickness gains momentum
    No cure, no quick relief
So many prayers unanswered
    Constant my gnawing grief

The tongues that lash, the words that cut
    With threats on every side
Bleeding and weak, I stagger on
    To reach the other side

Ah child, I hear each gasping breath
    I see your frightened clasp
I know you fear that you will sink
    You're at your final gasp

But if I said "the other side"
    Dear child, I'll take you there
There is no cause to doubt My Word
    No reason to despair!

Thy God Looks After Thee

"Be of good cheer," I see your burdened heart
    I know that there My healing touch must start
Repentance for your sin I clearly see
    Therefore, weak one, I take you unto Me

Oh glorious day—what greater day than this
    When Christ removed my sin and wretchedness
Forgiven, I rejoice to be His own
    His very blood for my sin did atone

Be of good cheer, although great tempests rage
    Be of good cheer, though life a tangled maze
I am right there, though you do not see Me
    Dear child, take heart, thy God looks after thee!

My Delight

"Why art thou cast down, O my soul? and why art thou disquieted within me? hope thou in God: for I shall yet praise him, who is the health of my countenance, and my God." Ps. 42:11

    His promises are my delight
        For they will never fail
    Though trials abound and storms may rage
        And foes against me rail

    "Be of good cheer," the Master cried
        "My Word shall be fulfilled"
    Those very words—balm to my soul
        My fears and doubts have stilled!

Submission

The greatest burden man can bear
　　Is sin, its weight untold
But Christ has died upon the cross
　　To bring me to His fold

He cries, "Come, hardened Christian
　　My blood is there for you
I'll take the burden off your back
　　Your heart and soul renew

Why labour after food and drink
　　That cannot satisfy
Your thirst remains, not filled at all
　　No matter how you try

'Tis only I that have the right
　　To forgive any man
For on the cross, God satisfied
　　With His redemption plan

Therefore, dear child, take up My yoke
    Submission to My will
Though it may lead to sorrows
    Your life with hardship fill

With My yoke there to guide you
    You'll find My burden light
As underneath its leading
    You'll do what I think right!"

Take it and all that it may hold
    With joy; yes, willingly
Because You know I'm sharing
    The weight of it with Thee!

Does My Faith Falter?

Does my faith dwindle, falter
    If I can't see ahead?
Clouds hiding the horizon
    Obscure what God hath said

Or do I lean on God's Word
    Knowing it standeth sure
Naught will fail that He promised
    Through all He will endure!

Patience

It's all very well to say we have faith
    When everything falls into place
But when disappointment and trouble abound
    It's patience we need in the race

Patience to trust God and rest in His will
    Patience that in our heart peace will instill
Patience just waits, though we can't understand
    Because we're holding right onto God's hand

Failure & Repentance

"The steps of a good man are ordered by the Lord: and he delighteth in his way. Though he fall, he shall not be utterly cast down: for the Lord upholdeth him with his hand."

Psalm 37:23–24

FRIENDSHIP WITH THE WORLD

I thought that I could still be friends
  With those from worldly days
I thought that I could influence them
  In many different ways

And so I went to places that
  A Christian should not be
And did some things that were not right
  To keep their love, you see

I found my love for God grow cold
  I did not search His Word
For in it He had pointed to
  The false friends I preferred

Within my heart His still small voice
  Had whispered, "Can this be
That you should take the hand of those
  Who hate and disown Me?"

Ah Lord, I turn my back upon
  The friends who abhor Thee
I'll pray for them, but will not let
  Them take my heart from Thee

I Did Not Take the Time

I did not take the time, dear Lord
    To read Thy precious Word
And thus my heart has colder grown
    My conscience not been stirred

I did not find the treasures
    That Thou had sent to me
Because I did not look for them
    In Thy Word, earnestly

I did not find Thy comfort
    I stumbled on the road
I groaned beneath my burdens
    I reaped as I had sowed

Ah Lord, my great neglecting
    Of Thee, Thy Word, Thy will
Has made Thy gentle whisper
    Become so deathly still

And thus I turn repentant
    I will redeem the time
I'll read Thy Word, obey it
    I'll treasure every line

DISOBEDIENCE

Dear Lord, I neglected to witness
    The cry of the lost, I ignored
But now I take up Thy commission
    To reach the unsaved, precious Lord

How sad—when I should have been silent
    I argued and spoke out of turn
Thy truths I flung down in great anger
    Naught could souls from me therefore learn

Dear Lord, Thou hast held out obedience
    To me as I walked on life's way
But I did not grasp it; I loathed it
    And wandered from Thee every day

Why Should I Not Be First?

Why should I not be first, dear Lord
  In all consideration?
Surely the rest should see that I
  Deserve their adulation!

I will not make an effort, Lord
  For others' "need of care"
After all that's spent on me
  Naught is left to spare!

I am not really selfish, Lord
  But people need to see
That life revolves conclusively
  And only around me!

I left the realms of heaven, child
  Was born a frail babe
I came to die upon the cross
  Your mortal soul to save

The King of kings was sacrificed
  To rid your life from sin
How can you stoop to selfishness
  And say you follow Him?

No Room for God, Oh Christian

No room for God, Oh Christian
    Your life has crowded grown
You filled it up with mundane things
    You govern it alone

The Master has been ousted
    Your heart He does not own
And so you selfishly stride on
    Wrapped in yourself alone

'Tis true the child of God may grieve
    The Spirit every day
Because in many areas
    He does not have full sway

The haunting words "No room" describes
    The tragedy that you
Have mapped your life and steered your course
    As captain, ship, and crew!

Make room, make room, Oh Christian
    Your Master pleads today
Your dreams, your plans, your friends, your time
    Before the Saviour lay

Bitterness

Ah Lord, this great sorrow and sickness
    The suffering I must embrace
Has made me embittered and angry
    It is clearly seen on my face

My child, you can let what I hold out
    Fall down to the ground and be lost
Or take what I've placed on your pathway
    Accepting the pain and the cost

Yes Lord, I will not let the burdens
    And callings fall down to the ground
But rather allow them to make me
    A blessing wherever I'm found

I Used to Trust Thy Word

I used to trust Thy Word, Oh Lord
    It was my strength and stay
But then I lost my confidence
    And stumbled on my way

The promises that used to keep
    My faith buoyant and strong
Are not the same, for I'm scared that
    To me they don't belong

I've disappointed Thee, dear Lord
    And thus I am afraid
To clasp Thy Word, rely on it
    From Thee, Thy child hath strayed

Ah precious one, how can you spurn
    My Word that speaks to thee
That brings the light, points out the way
    Into eternity

It shows your sin is paid for
    Points to My sacrifice
Describes how you can conquer
    O'er evil, sin, and vice

It tells of My compassion
    Forgiveness and My love
My tenderness to carry
    My lambs to heaven above

Dear Lord, Thy Word I'll treasure
    With confidence I'll read
For in it Thou hast promised
    To meet my every need

My Confidence Has Slipped

Dear Lord, I let my confidence
    In Thee, Thy Word, Thy power
Slip from my fingers in this year
    And thus my life turned sour

My joy in Thy salvation
    The peace that is within
Had disappeared as doubt crept in
    And doubting Thee is sin

Thus in exasperation
    I flung my trust away
I did not lean on Thee at all
    To be my strength and stay

Because dark doubt had tiptoed in
    My heart met dark despair
For in the darkness Thy own light
    Was dim, drowned out by care

But now, dear Lord, I come to Thee
    Confessing doubts and fear
To Thee, who ruleth over all
    Thy faltering child draws near

I know my God in heaven
    Is sovereign over all
I will not doubt His goodness
    Though hardships o'er me fall

This life is but a passage
    To heaven, where at last
I'll understand God's dealings
    Pain, tears, and trials past

Thus confidence I'll take up
    I'll not cast it away
For my Redeemer liveth
    I'll trust Him every day

Dear Lord

Dear Lord, I fear my hands will be
Empty on judgment day
Because my feet were loathe to go
And point souls to Thy way

Too Proud, Child of Mine

Too proud to acknowledge, child of Mine
    The error of your way
Too proud to turn, come back to Me
    From where your feet did stray

Too proud to submit to authority
    Too haughty to obey
Thus you are stumbling on your path
    And crippled every day

I Took a Little Sin

Dear Lord, I took a little sin
    To come and dwell with me
So small it wasn't seen at all
    And hid from all, but Thee!

But now this little sin has grown
    And robbed me of my joy
It has become my master
    I am in its employ

My child, you cannot harbour sin
    Without a consequence
You'll steep your life in misery
    And lose your confidence

Repent in earnest penitence
    Seek My forgiveness true
I'll wash away that monstrous sin
    That's busy ruining you!

It Started Subtly

Dear Lord, it started subtly
    With just a lie or two
I was in a dilemma
    It seemed the thing to do

I was in a tight corner
    The only escape path
Was to resort to white lies
    Not to be drowned with wrath

But now my armour's useless
    As vulnerable I face
The enemy who knows "Truth"
    Is not girdled in place

Ah, cleanse me from the inside
    That in my inward part
There is no place for deceit
    But a pure, upright heart

UNKIND

Sadly unkind to parents, brothers, sisters
    In word and deed, hurting them every day
So many things that could have eased their burdens
    I've left undone upon my selfish way

I did not heed God's gentle, earnest pleading
    That I should love, forgive, be tender, kind
If I neglect God's clear and strict injunctions
    I to His mercy will be cruelly blind

Did He not pay for sin the total ransom?
    With His own blood the sacrifice was made
His body bruised and battered, scourged and broken
    For me His form upon the cross was laid

Can I who humbly sought the Lord's forgiveness
    Keep back my own from those who anger me?
Can I who tasted mercy and compassion
    Towards a brother, sister, wrathful be?

My Protection

Why did you not heed My call, precious wand'rer?
    There where you walk 'neath the judgment of sin
Time and again has My soft voice been calling
    You to repentance—your soul would I win

But you have left My protection—foolhardy
    You who were once 'neath My sheltering wing
See how the elements rage in their fury
    I would, My fallen one, you to Me bring

You who are fearful and quivering in torment
    Who still—despite My concern and My care
Fear the fierce anger that men are inflicting
    Rest in the knowledge that I'm always there

There to sustain and to nourish, to cherish
    There to stir up when I want you to fly
There to encourage as feebly you flutter
    There to bear heavenwards, child, when you die

My Great Failure

How can I be a witness
How can I be a light
When my great failure hovers
Never quite out of sight?

No one can see God's beauty
Past my enormous scar
That failure—life o'ershadows
My testimony doth mar

Don't let the faults of bygones
    Rob you of fruit today
Don't let it mar your image
    Haunt you upon life's way

Ah child, your King is sovereign
    He'll cleanse repented sin
His sweet forgiveness granted
    Doth His acceptance bring

Don't let the faults of bygones
    Rob you of fruit today
Rather seek God's forgiveness
    To wash your sins away

So that the faults of bygones
    Buried, discarded are
Letting you advance forward
    Without a crippling scar

THINGS HAVE GONE WRONG

Things have gone wrong, weary pilgrim
    Can it be sin at your door?
Judgment hath heavily fallen
    Seek God, His mercy implore

Things have gone wrong, but life's transient
    Heaven awaits further on
Lift up your eyes, He is coming
    Rest your hard lot thereupon

Things have gone wrong; men are watching
    Will you victorious be?
Will they seek God by your actions
    What will their silent eyes see?

Things have gone wrong; Satan's gloating
    You will not stand this great trial
But heaven looks for endurance
    God's grace to traverse each mile

Things have gone wrong; are you trying
    To work things outside God's will
Blocking His persistent warnings
    Will you God's tender voice still?

Things have gone wrong; seek the answer
    Can you with confidence say
They were not born of your doing
    Your conscience clear on this day?

If so—dear child, rest your burdens
    Full on your dear Saviour's breast
There you will find His enabling
    Child, to survive every test

This Modern World

It's tempting in this modern world
    To skim the edge of sin
To seek the world's approval
    Desire her smile to win

It seems so hard to be the one
    That's always saying "no"
To what the world deems reasonable
    It aggravates them so

And thus I'm tempted to go down
    The lanes that God abhors
While Satan's music fills my ears
    I cross forbidden doors

I've ended up so miserable
    I've questioned life—its aims
Because I dabbled with the world
    Down many hell-bound lanes!

Why Should I Make an Effort?

Why should I make an effort
    Exert myself each day
When I could be reclining
    And slouch upon life's way?

One day when I reach heaven
    What shame will fill my breast
That I had been so lazy
    Not given of my best

How can I meet my Saviour
    Knowing that I've misused
The precious time He's given
    Lazily it abused?

Let me redeem the moments
    Given by God to me
Work in the time allotted
    Fulfill my destiny

Voices Keep Calling God's Children

Voices keep calling God's children
  To wander from His way
Images keep on appearing
  Seeking their will to sway

Does the way seem too stony?
  Is the path very rough?
Does your whole being cry out
  "Surely it is too tough"?

Do the world's lights allure you?
    Have you turned from the plough?
Is your light burning dimly?
    Stop!—seek your Master now

Perhaps it is wealth and power
    Or just a life of ease
Satan has many draw cards
    By which he aims to please

Demas had left the pathway
    Satan had gained his goal
When Paul's mourned fellow worker
    Let the world rob his soul

Flee from the tempter's whispers
    Cling to the narrow way
That you can face your Maker
    On the Great Judgment Day

I Murmured

Dear God, Thy child did murmur
    She embraced discontent
Dissatisfied with others
    Her lot, though by Thee sent

She did not count all her blessings
    She did not perceive that Thou
Had showered her with goodness
    With mercy did endow

Until she was awakened
    To see another's woe
To stand beside a sister
    Her deeper sorrows know

And thus Thy child was humbled
    Ashamed of discontent
She bows in deep submission
    To Thy will she is bent

Too Great is the Cost

God has been telling me to reach the lost
    But at the moment, too great is the cost
I am not reckless, but life is so dear
    Let me postpone it 'till old age is here

There is a visit I know I should make
    I have a mandate to do for Christ's sake
But there are things more important to me
    Before the poor soul I'll visit for Thee

Time passes quietly and slips out of sight
    While we procrastinate to do the right
Ah, what deep sorrow will grip us at last
    When time is ended and chances are past

Ashamed!

I feel ashamed when I think back
   Of what was seen in me
Sadly, others will not reply
   That I have been godly

Instead of seeking to please God
   In every single way
I did just as I pleased, therefore
   People provoked each day!

Oh Lord, I must confess that I
   Have fallen into sin
I fear that those who know me now
   Will be harder to win

Cleanse me, dear Lord, I wish to grow
   More godly every day
To be a light, not stumbling block
   To others on my way!

Sadly Lacking

There are the Christians who have
    Been saved; we know it's true
But wisdom sadly lacking
    In what they say and do!

Not wise, how sad the verdict
    On such a stagnant heart
Not reaching their potential
    Planned for them from the start!

The Christian's Calling

"Let your light so shine before men, that they may see your good works, and glorify your Father which is in heaven."

Matthew 5:16

The Poor Man

The poor man on the country road
Battered, bleeding, spent
Cried for help to the passers-by
Several past him went

A priest came by with pious mien
He must have seen the man
For swift he turned his head away
And almost from him ran

The footsteps of the Pharisee
With head in haughty pose
Too passed him with averted eyes
Compassion in him froze

And then the dear Samaritan
Reached out with loving care
For in the smallest detail
Nothing would he spare

Do I pass by those suffering
And avert my eyes
Shut my ears as I go by
To their needs and cries?

Ah, forgive my tardiness
And my lack of zeal
I take up my calling, Lord
To the lost's appeal

Satan's Legions

Satan with all his legions
    Would God's work hurt, oppose
In prayer we stand against him
    The door against him close

HAVE YOU PURPOSED?

Daniel had landed in foreign soil
    Heathen would him in their toils embroil
Temptations came to deny the Lord
    "Do what we tell you!" their voices roared

We too seem sunk in a world of sin
    We can't escape all the sordid din
At work or school, the incessant cry
    "Join us; 'tis naught if you God deny!"

Daniel had purposed he would not yield
    To their attractions; his soul was steeled
Thus he said "no" when the call was made
    Daniel determined, had faithful stayed

Have you too purposed to not deny
    Christ though the battle is raging high?
Child of the kingdom, like Daniel say
    "I will not yield to the tempter's sway."

There Is No Better Time

There are so many arguments
    Of dates and source and rights
That mingles with this Christmas time
    And its commercial lights

We sometimes miss the chance that Paul
    Had grabbed so long ago
When he had used the "unknown god"
    To point to God below

So much is wrong, the sceptics claim
    In all this celebration
But do they take the time to point
    The world to Christ's salvation?

There is no better time to show
    The reason that He came
His birth, death, resurrection
    Redemption in His name

How can we cling to prejudice
    And miss the chance each year
To sing His praise from grateful hearts
    For this lost world to hear?

I Always Dreamt

I always dreamt what I should be
From childhood 'till today
Somehow I mapped a certain path
Career, to mark my way

But suddenly the Master came
And said, "Child, follow Me
The work that I planned long ago
I do assign to thee."

So different from the dreams that I
Had dreamt of long ago
And thus the plan God had for me
Descended like a blow

Dear God, acclaimed within this world
Thy child should surely be
It cannot be that Thou would call
Him for a missionary

How sad to shut the Master out
From plans and dreams that we
Without Him set in motion
On their sad destiny

Ambassador

Ambassador, ambassador
    God made my calling clear
To be His representative
    Upon this earthly sphere

My dress, my speech, my attitude
    A pointer to God's will
So that a hunger for His realm
    The seeking souls will fill

The Breastplate

The breastplate that God gives us
    His own pure righteousness
Will help me in the warfare
    Though sore the crisis is

How can I let this breastplate
    Be stained by my weak sin
I'll keep it pure and holy
    That I won't lose—but win!

I Had Left Thy Sword

This morning I had left Thy sword
    Not grabbed it eagerly
Thus I was powerless to stop
    My mortal enemy

At night, dear Lord, my sword is gone
    Instead of keeping it
Right next to me, it was not there
    I now defeated sit

Child, fierce the battle's raging
    You need to grip your sword
Formidable the enemy
    Whose wrath on you is poured

This Morning

This morning on these camp grounds
    We're in the midst of war
But with Christ as our Captain
    We don't fear anymore!

Our armour tightly fitted
    We call on God today
To lead us into battle
    To conquer in the fray

Though Satan would oppose us
    We don't give up the fight
We'll pray and keep on praying
    'Till victory is in sight

God Has Equipped Us

God has equipped us for the fight
    With armies from on high
So that we need not fear and flee
    When Satan standeth nigh

But clasp your armour tightly
    Hold up your shield so true
Then grip your sword to face the foe
    And victory will ensue!

The World Is Ever Clinging

<pre>
The world is ever clinging
    She'll not give up her own
We'll fight her on the prayer front
    'Till off her feet she's blown
</pre>

I See the Enemy

Dear Lord, I see the enemy
    Lurk from my rampart wall
And thus I call, I cry to Thee
    "Come help me, lest I fall."

On all fronts, Satan's busy
    He's here to wreck, destroy
But I stand to oppose him
    My weapons I'll employ

Formidable the onslaught
    Yes, fierce the enemy
But powerless to conquer
    If Thou art leading me

Oh, Dangerous to Go Right In

Oh, dangerous to go right in
    The fierce forefront of war
If you cannot be certain
    Your Captain goes before

The helmet of salvation
    Must be a genuine one
For prayer to be effective
    For battles to be won!

The Battle Is a Fierce One

The battle is a fierce one
    As we engage in prayer
While Satan and his allies
    Would bring us to despair

We feel so weak and helpless
    To fight against this foe
But faith bids us consider
    That Christ has laid him low

Thus we need not be vanquished
    Nor timid to engage
The enemy on all sides
    Nor shrink beneath his rage

For Christ is at the forefront
    We march forth in His name
God's soldier in God's army
    The victory we claim!

Judgment & the Unsaved

"For the invisible things of him from the creation of the world are clearly seen, being understood by the things that are made, even his eternal power and Godhead; so that they are without excuse:"

Romans 1:20

"And as it is appointed unto men once to die, but after this the judgment:"

Hebrews 9:27

Too Proud

Too proud to acknowledge your need of God
    Too proud to bow to Him
Too proud to turn from depravity
    From waywardness and sin

Thus, lost without God, eternally
    Your soul in turmoil lands
Because your pride had closed the door
    And barred God's helping hand

You Spurned My Love

When My arms said, "Come to Me"
You merely crossed your own
My love lay shattered at your feet
Your heart as hard as stone

You did not grasp My proffered love
You spurned My sacrifice
You chose to turn and walk away
Embraced a life of vice

But one day at the judgment throne
My book shall opened be
Then sorrowfully you'll recognize
You have no part in Me

You let My love fall to the ground
You spurned it 'neath your feet
And thus condemned and sent to hell
Before the judgment seat

No Room—the Agnostic and Sceptic

"No room for God," the sceptic says
    In this enlightened age
"God is a figment of the mind
    Developed stage by stage."

"No room for God," the agnostic cries
    "He is a myth of man
This fleeting life will end in death
    An earthbound, human span."

No room for God—what awakening
    When he stands at God's throne
To face God's wrath and judgment
    He'll writhe and cry and groan

Procrastination

    I am not hardened to God and His ways
        I'll seek His pardon in more distant days
    This is the time to live life to the brim
        Why should I repent and finish with sin?

    Then a loud screeching and slamming of brakes
        A crumpled vehicle—'tis all that it takes
    Procrastinator, you'll weep as you cry
        "Why did I spurn God, my chances deny?"

At the Judgment Seat

There at the judgment seat of Christ
    Will my eyes shed bitter tears
For the souls that I neglected
    Down countless wasted years?

Were there questions I avoided?
    Were there longings I ignored?
Did I fear mankind's rejection
    And thus deny Thee, Lord?

Ah, what bitter sighs and moaning
    Ah, what cries for chances lost
When I see my blessed Saviour
    And perceive salvation's cost

He had come from heaven's glory
    Down to earth, to suffer, die
So that man could be forgiven
    "It is finished," was His cry

He has risen, gone to glory
    And doth ask His children true
To take up the precious gospel
    Hold it out—for Him anew

Can we let the lost go swiftly
    Without warning into hell?
Are we faithful in our witness
    Will regret our bosom fill?

Will you take up the commission
    To God's calling faithful be
As a light and as a witness
    Impact others' destiny?

No Room

Man, you resist God, His calling
    Stilling His voice every day
Suppressing, hardening your conscience
    Heedlessly going your way

Fainter the sight of His mercy
    Farther His grace doth recede
Dimmer the sense of your frailty
    Deadened the sense of your need

Until your life's thread is ended
    Time passed to be never more
And the word "while" gains momentum
    As you face heaven's closed door

No room on earth for your Saviour
    No room for His gentle voice
No room to turn back, O Sinner
    No room has sealed your own choice

STORIES FROM SCRIPTURE

What they taught us

SHADRACH, MESHACH, ABEDNEGO

Shadrach and Meshach, Abednego
    Stood when the others were falling low
Knowing that death was the price they'd pay
    If they were faithful to God that day

Drums rolled, the cry rang to bend the knee
    Before the image—a King's decree
But they were willing to burn and die
    God alone honour and not deny

You too are called forth to bend the knee
    Be it at school, child, or 'varsity
Life will be death if you don't comply
    Compromise beckons to bend or die

Shadrach and Meshach, Abednego
    Glorified God many years ago
Christ was with them in the scorching flames
    Tested, they stood—glorified His name

What will you do, child, decide today
    Will you give in to the world's dark sway?
Or will you stand up, not bend the knee
    Succumb to pressure—but faithful be?

Dark Clouds Around Daniel

Dark clouds were gathering 'round Daniel that day
   Hinting that he should depart from God's way
Should he obey if his life was at risk?
   Lions that are hungry make dinner quite brisk!

Daniel was threatened, would he compromise
   Secretly pray, hid from men's prying eyes?
No, he was faithful, he did as before
   Honouring God, though men stood at the door

He was arrested, his punishment came
   Thrown in the pit with the lions far from tame
God sent an angel to safeguard His child
   Muzzled the lions sat, both placid and mild

Daniel was faithful, thus he passed the test
   He did not falter, shame God, like the rest
Will I be faithful when things go so wrong?
   Showing, like Daniel, to Whom I belong

Among the Shouting Crowd

She lay among the shouting crowd
    Condemned, accused, despised
A woman who had stooped so low
    "Kill her!" the angry cries

But then the Saviour came, drew near
    He gazed upon their rage
Read the life-book of their lives
    Each self-righteous page

    Bending and writing in the sand
        Men did blush for shame
    Was it hidden sin exposed
        Written there by name?

    "He that hath no sin," saith He
        Had the right to throw
    Stones upon this wretched soul
        Cowered here below

    Stealthily they slunk away
        Guilt had silenced them
    Then the Master turned to her
        "Child, I'll not condemn

    But I call thee to repent
        Go and sin no more
    From the darkness to the light
        Pass—I am the door!"

When I Look at Peter

When I look at Peter
>   Who failed so publicly
It would seem he never
>   Could be a testimony

After all, the Peter
>   We read of in God's Word
Swore and denied Jesus
>   And the gathered crowd had heard

Then the eager cockerel
>   Had crowed with lusty lung
Stirring Peter's conscience
>   His repentance had begun

Peter was so humbled
>   Looking at Jesus' eyes
He went outside weeping
>   For pardon he had cried

Ah, the tender mercies
    Of our gracious Lord
That forgave poor Peter
    He was totally restored

But he'd be more patient
    With other erring souls
No more boasting arrogance
    Not master in control

Thus, though poor old Peter
    Failed hopelessly that day
His sin was forgiven
    Put behind him on life's way

Hannah and Samuel's Coat

Dear Lord, I am working upon a coat
    For the child I gave to Thee
How I miss his little feet
    Tripping right close to me

Lord, in the stitches are hidden prayers
    For the safety of my boy
Knowing that in Thy home, dear Lord
    He walks in Thy employ

But there are hidden dangers, Lord
    Even within Thy house
Hophni and Phinehas play with sin
    And others would entice

Thus keep my darling close to Thee
    Warn him to walk aright
May he choose the better way
    And only do what's right

THE LORD HAS ANSWERED PRAYER
Hannah

The Lord has mercif'ly answered prayer
    And showered me with love
Turned my weeping into joy
    Bent down from heaven above

Once I walked with downcast mien
    Now with constant praise
I lift my face up unto God
    Within my altered ways

God has mercif'ly answered prayer
    Bless His holy name
Let the earth His praises sing
    And His might proclaim

LET US PULL OUT THE TARES

"But he said, Nay; lest while ye gather up the tares, ye root up also the wheat with them." Matt. 13:29

"Judge not, that ye be not judged. For with what judgment ye judge, ye shall be judged: and with what measure ye mete, it shall be measured to you again." Matt. 7:1–2

Dear Lord, let us pull out the tares
    The eager servants cried
We can't accept an alien plant
    It should not stay, abide

We're very able, Lord, to judge
    Those tares identify
Thus let us rip them from the field
    Thy crop to purify

Wait, wait, the Master cried, don't touch
    Or pull a single tare
For you see with a human eye
    A superficial stare!

I see beneath the outward form
    Into the human heart
My workings there you can't perceive
    Don't pull it all apart

Remember those who judge, condemn
    Will fall a prey in turn
Don't touch the Lord's anointed
    The Master's voice was stern

Leah Was Not Beautiful

Leah was not beautiful
    Her sister was the one
For beauty cherished, loved, preferred
    Whom Jacob's heart had won

But Leah had a tender eye
    We know that from God's Word
Despite her trials, rejections, hurt
    Her heart with pity stirred

A Child Ambassador
Naaman's slave girl

Tiny little captive in a foreign land
    In the household stranger; much to understand
Mother, father nowhere—small alone to be
    Strong enough to survive; be a testimony

Tiny little captive, you were upright, true
    Diligent in work; child, we should honour you
Ready to be pointing to your God above
    Child, you led that household to the realms above!

The Samaritan Woman

Her heart was filled with sin and mire
    With bitterness and hate
We all know of the life she led
    Her fallen, low-down state

No one knew all the misery
    That filled her lonely heart
Or how she longed that she could make
    A clean and wholesome start

Alone she drew her water
    Beneath the midday sun
For all and sundry knew her deeds
    And therefore, her did shun

But then the Master came, Who knew
    Why she had fallen low
And why she embraced misery
    Her heartache He did know

To her He offered pardon
    Himself: the Water true
So that this broken vessel
    Could be remade anew

Where sin had filled her being
    The Living Water sped
And washed each murky corner
    By what the Master said